Maritime Dynasty

History of the Griffiths Family

By Iolo Wyn Griffiths

About the Author

Iolo is a Community Content Curator with a group of newspapers in North Wales, and is keenly interested in genealogy and the local history of North Wales. His other publications include *A History of Beaumaris* (published in 2004), and four books, *A History of Beaumaris* (revised version), *A History of Bangor*, *A History of Amlwch*, *A History of Holyhead*, and *History of Conwy*, all of which are available both as ebooks on Kindle, and for print on demand on CreateSpace.

Cover Picture: William Griffiths (1864-1959) and his wife Ellen (née Thomas).

Table of Contents

Introduction

This book covers three generations of the Griffiths family, and over a century of maritime history. Major themes of this account are the strong maritime tradition of the village of Nefyn on the north coast of the Llŷn peninsula, the development of Liverpool as the capital of North Wales, and an important centre for emigration, and the exports of slates from Port Penrhyn, in Bangor.

This book will also look at some of the sources available for tracing the careers of mariners.

The early years of the family

Nefyn, on the north coast of the Llŷn Peninsula, provides an excellent natural harbour, defended from the west by the promontory of Porthdinllaen, and on the east by Penrhyn Nefyn. Although agriculture is an important industry, the land is too rugged to provide a satisfactory living for large families, and so herring fishing has traditionally supplemented the livelihoods of small landholders.

The fishing industry is of great antiquity, as inventories from as early as 1287 list people who possessed nets and boats, and as late as the early 19th century Nefyn had about 40 fishing boats, each owned by about seven persons, who would be usually farmers, tradesmen or sailors, but during the herring season, usually September to January, they would fish for herring, and the herring around Nefyn were of better quality than those from Cardigan Bay.

This dependence on the sea later led to Nefyn being a very important cradle of mariners, and it has been claimed that Nefyn and Porthdinllaen could claim more master mariners per square inch than any other part of the United Kingdom. It is therefore no surprise that at least three generations of the Griffiths family described in this book were mariners, and they can be regarded as a typical dynasty of seafarers.

However the recorded story of this family starts in Chester. On 17 September 1788, a William was christened at St Mary's church, of that city, the illegitimate son of a William Leech and Anne Griffith. The register of mariners in the Public Records Office in Kew gives the date of birth of William Griffiths as 15 August 1786, but I believe this should be 1788.

What happened to William Leach and Anne Griffith is unclear, but on 6 May 1790 an Anne Griffith, spinster married a William Griffith, cordwainer at St Mary's, and on 27 January 1793 a William Leech married an Elizabeth Ashton at St John the Baptist, Chester. It is not definite if these are the same ones as the parents of the William christened in 1788, as we are dealing with names that are fairly common in the area.

It is not known when William moved to the Nefyn area, as the clues available are rather sparse, but as Griffiths is a very common name there it may well be that his mother may have had some connection and moved back there. The register for his seaman's ticket in 1846 says that he first went to sea as an apprentice in 1803, when he was 15 years old, but it is not stated whether this was from Nefyn Chester, or elsewhere, or what ship he was on.

There is, however, no doubt that he was at Nefyn by 10 July 1813 when he married Eleanor Jones the daughter of William Jones and his wife Sydney, at Nefyn parish church. They were both said to be of Nefyn, and both made a mark.

Their children, all christened in Nefyn Parish church, were Hugh, christened 25 September 1814, Elinor, christened 29 June 1817, John, born 22 March 1820, and christened 9 March 1820, Robert, christened 10 October 1824 and Sydney, christened 18 August 1827.

In 1844 a system was introduced whereby any seaman leaving the UK was required to have a register ticket. The National Archives in Kew, London, has the registers and indexes to these tickets (BT 113 and 114). William received his registration ticket number 65, 837 at Bristol, on 24 December 1846, and the register gives a few tantalising clues about some of his voyages in the 1840s. In 1845 and the first half of 1846 he sailed on ship 702-117, while in the second half of 1846 and all of 1847 and 1848 he sailed on ship 755-117. The number 117 represents the port, in this case Caernarfon (which also covered Pwllheli and Barmouth). The numbers 702 and 755 represent the ships, but in the absence of a key to these numbers, this does not help us much.

What does add much interest is the detailed description of the sailor. The ticketing system was introduced as a means of keeping records of seamen, and in a hazardous occupation where a man may be lost at sea, it would be helpful to have a record of their general description and any marks, so that it would be possible to identify any bodies found at sea. This system eventually collapsed under the weight of the bureaucracy it required, and ceased in 1853.

William Griffiths was 5ft 3 tall, had a sallow complexion, black hair, hazel eyes, and no distinctive marks. He had not served in the Royal Navy or in foreign service, and could not write.

However in 1849 and 1850 no voyages are reported, but in 1851 he sailed on ship 755 both halves of the year, and on March 30 1851 appears on the census for Llain Madryn, Morfa Nefyn, with his wife, and his birthplace is given as Nefyn, and in 1861 as retired mariner, born in Chester, England, with his widowed daughter Sydney Evans, and grandson William Evans.

We shall return to William when we examine the intricate share dealings which he and his son John, and his daughter Sydney, had with the Eleanor and Jane.

John Griffiths (1820-1890)

John Griffiths, who was born on 22 March 1820, first went to sea as a boy on 24 March 1835 on the *Newhope* of Pwllheli (40 tons) where he was until the December of that year. The details of his service up to 1851 is recorded on his application for his Master's Certificate, and gives a good start for tracing his career.

From 3 April 1836 to 23 November 1838 he was a boy on another Pwllheli ship (50 tons) but the name of this ship is difficult to read on his master's certificate, which is my source for his early service. His service on both these ships was in the coasting trade that covered Great Britain, Ireland, France north of Brest, and to the Elbe.

From 5 March to 29 November, 1839 he was a seaman on the *Madryn*, a schooner of 75 tons of Pwllheli. JJ Thomas of Nefyn, for John Parry of Nefyn, built the *Madryn* at Nefyn in 1836. Its dimensions were 54.9ft by 17.3ft by 10.4ft. While we don't have details of this voyage, 19th century local newspapers often carried a Shipping Intelligence column for ships arriving and leaving local ports. In this particular case the *North Wales Chronicle* of 7 May 1839, refers to the *Madryn* (Capt Roberts), clearing Port Penrhyn, Bangor, thus referring to one of the ports of call, and we can guess that slates would very likely have formed the cargo in this case. Port Penrhyn was taken over and expanded by Lord Penrhyn in 1786, so as to provide an outlet for his slate quarries, and this seems to have been the main trade of this port.

The National Library of Wales's database Welsh Newspapers Online provides the means for searching Welsh newspapers between 1804 and 1919, and makes it easy to track down the references to the ships' ports of call. In the case of the ships that John would have sailed on, the *North Wales Chronicle* and the *Carnarvon and Denbigh Herald* are the main sources of information. Since the information is usually on the arrival and departure from local ports, and only occasionally refer to the ports further afield that the ships were arriving from or sailing to, the picture is a string of snapshots.

From 6 January 1840 to 27 January 1841 he was a Seaman on *Diligence* of Pwllheli (130 tons) in coasting trade. The *Diligence* was registered in 1816 and built at Barmouth, and its length was 590 feet, breadth 20 feet, depth 11 feet in hold. Its rigging was described as snow, and had a square stern. Tracing the movements of this ship from the newpaper reports is complicated by the fact that *Diligence* appears to have been a very popular name for ships of that name captained by masters with the surnames Bydder, Rees, Jones and Edwards calling at Caernarfon and Bangor (and the Crew List Indexing Project lists 32 ships of that name). Ships are identified in the Shipping Intelligence columns at that time by the name of the captain. In this case it will be vain to try to identify the right ship without more information.

From 10 February 1841 to 6 December 1845 he was Mate on *Reindeer* (80 tons) of Pwllheli in the coasting trade, whose rotation number in 1845 was 602. At least here the cryptic details given in the seamen's register are supplemented by John's later application for a Master's certificate, so that we can know which ship 602 refers to.

The *Reindeer* was a 75-ton schooner built by H Roberts in 1841 for Robert Hughes of Nefyn. Its dimensions were 57.8 feet by 18.2 feet by 10.4 feet. Griffith Hughes, Methodist minister at Edern and son of Captain John Hughes of the *Palmyra*, held 2/64th shares in the *Reindeer* (Pwllheli Register 2 of 1849).

The Shipping Intelligence columns in the *Carnarvon and Denbigh Herald* and the *North Wales Chronicle* gives some limited information about the voyages of the *Reindeer*, specifically arrivals and departures from three local ports, namely Port Penrhyn (Bangor), Caernarfon, and Porthdinllaen, and between August 1841 and September 1843 the Captain is called Hughes.

By May 1844 the ship is commanded by a Captain Griffiths, with the same ports of call being named in the newspaper reports. While it might be tempting to think that John Griffiths had been promoted from being Mate on the *Reindeer*, this is unlikely to be the case, as the *Reindeer* was still under Captain

Griffiths as late as at least 1853, long after John became Master of the *Ellen and Ann* in 1846.

On 17 January 1845 he received his registration ticket (number 12,111) at London. He was described as a seaman, height 5ft 3, hair brown, complexion dark, eyes grey, no marks. He had not served in Royal Navy or in foreign service. When unemployed he resided at Nefyn and could write.

From 9 April 1846 to 27 January 1851 he was the Master of the *Ellen and Ann* of Pwllheli (32 tons) in the coasting trade. In 1847 the rotation number of the *Ellen and Ann* in the port of Caernarfon was 102. (In this particular case again the details given on his application for his Master's Certificate, and the details in the register for his registration ticket allows me to deduce the identity of the ship involved). It seems that Port Penrhyn, Bangor is a very regular port of call, mentioned in the *Carnarvon and Denbigh Herald* on 20 June 1846, the *North Wales Chronicle* on 1 September 1846 (the *Ellen and Ann* was mentioned in the *Carnarvon and Denbigh Herald* of 29 August as passing through the Menai Strait, clearly on her way to Bangor), and the *Carnarvon and Denbigh Herald* of 10 October 1846.

The only reference found to a voyage in 1847 in Welsh Newspapers Online comes from a South Wales newspaper, the *Monmouthshire Merlin*, of 3 July, referring to the *Ellen and Ann* sailing from Newport to Liverpool, so we get a hint at a voyage further afield.

Some of the references in the *Carnarvon and Denbigh Herald* to 1848 voyages also give more detail, with the 15 January edition mentioning the Ellen and Ann arriving at Caernarfon on 11 January from Runcorn, and the 19 February mentioning her passing through the Menai Strait on 17 February from Bangor to Arundel.

CARNARVON CASTLE AND TOWN.

Illustration 1: The port of Caernarfon in the 1850s

The *Carnarvon and Denbigh Herald* on both 15 April and 22 April mentioning arriving at Porthdinllaen. This begs the question of whether this is the same arrival mentioned twice, or had there been a very short, very local voyage in the meantime. As Porthdinllaen is very near to his home in Morfa Nefyn (very likely he was living at Llain Madryn, which was his address in September 1848), it would be natural for this to be a port to which he would return.

The *Carnarvon and Denbigh Herald* of 15 July 1848 is a case where the ship's destination after departing is given, with the *Ellen and Ann* sailing from Caernarfon on 10 July to Newry.

On 26 August 1848 the *Carnarvon and Denbigh Herald* refers to the *Ellen and Ann* arriving at Port Penrhyn.

On 8 September 1848 he married Jane Williams of Cwmistir Bach, the daughter of William and Catherine Williams, at Edern Parish church. He then lived at Llain Madryn, Morfa Nefyn. Their children were Sydney (born 1849), Catherine (born 1850), Jane (born 1854), Ann (born 1858), and William (born 30 September 1864, and christened at Garn Fadrun, by the rites of the Calvinistic Methodists, on 26 November 1865, when his parents lived at Tyn Rhos, Morfa Nefyn).

His voyages on the *Ellen and Ann* after he got married are again followed by the Shipping Intelligence columns of the *Carnarvon and Denbigh Herald*, with references to sailing from Porthdinllaen (18 November 1848), clearing out of Port Penrhyn, Bangor with slates (1 September 1849), sailing from Porthdinllaen (8 September 1849), sailing from Port Penrhyn (8 December 1849).

On 27 April 1850, there is reference to the *Ellen and Ann* passing through the Menai Strait on 22 April, going from Bangor to Southampton. Since we often find references to ships sailing from Port Penrhyn in the Shipping columns being followed by the remark "all with slates", it can be presumed that this is the usual cargo from Bangor.

The series of snapshots continues with references to arriving at Port Penrhyn (22 June 1850), arriving at Porthdinllaen (27 July 1850), arriving at Port Penrhyn again (7 September 1850), and sailing from Caernarfon to Bristol (28 September 1850). Dates in bracklets are those of the newspapers which carry the relevant Shipping Intelligence columns.

Both the *North Wales Chronicle* and the *Carnarvon and Denbigh Herald* on 12 October 1850 mention the *Ellen and Ann* arriving at, and sailing from Porthdinllaen.

In the first half of 1851 he sailed on the ship numbered 799 of the port of Caernarfon. When we have deduced that the rotation number of the *Ellen and Ann* is 102, this is a bit of a mystery. Had the ship somehow been renumbered, or was he temporarily on another ship? The known voyages found in the Shipping Intelligence columns in February and April 1851 were on the *Ellen and Ann*.

On 27 January 1851 he applied for Master's Certificate of Service, at Edern, Caernarfonshire. He then resided at Edern, while the census on March 30 shows that this was specifically Cwmistir Bach, the home of his in-laws. The witness was Griffith Roberts of Edern. His certificate, numbered 40,532 was issued at Pwllheli on 13 May 1851.

During February and April the snapshots given of his voyages are that on 14 February, the *Ellen and Ann* was at Caernarfon before sailing for Bristol, and that on 10 April she arrived at Barmouth from Cardiff, and on 16 April sailed from Porthdinllaen. We can deduce that the *Ellen and Ann* was in the coasting trade, as even the ports further afield named are all British.

Subsequent Shipping Intelligence columns refer to sailing from Porthdinllaen (24 May 1851), arriving in Caernarfon on 10 August (14 August, 1851), sailing from Caernarfon to Newport on 28 August (30 August 1851), arriving in Caernarfon from Newry on 30 September (4 October 1851), arriving at Port Penrhyn (30 October 1851), sailing from Caernarfon (27 November 1851), arriving at Caernarfon from Swansea on 17 December (20 December 1851).

Voyages in 1852 follow a similar pattern, sailing from Caernarfon to Swansea on 19 February (21 February 1852), arriving at Caernarfon from Swansea, 11 March (13 March 1852), arriving at Caernarfon on 16 March (18 March 1852, so presumably there must have been a very short voyage between 11 March and 16 March), sailing from Porthdinllaen (20 March 1852), sailing from

Caernarfon (7 May 1852), arriving at Caernarfon from Porthdinllaen, 17 May (22 May 1852).

The snapshots of 1853 voyages, include arriving at Caernarfon on 9 March (11 March 1853), sailing from Port Penrhyn (1 April 1853), arrival at Porthdinllaen, 24 May (27 May 1853), arrival at Caernarfon, 15 June (17 June 1853), sailing from Caernarfon on 22 June (24 June 1853), arrival at Port Penrhyn, Bangor (27 August 1853), arrival at Caernarfon 27 October (29 October 1853).

His 1854 voyages including arriving at Porthmadog on 26 January (28 January 1854). The North Wales Chronicle of 11 March 1854 reports the *Ellen and Ann* arriving and sailing from Porthdinllaen on 8 March, and arriving at Porthmadog on 9 March.

On 8 April, 1854 the *North Wales Chronicle* reports the *Ellen and Ann* sailing from Porthmadog. It is difficult to think that the ship remained at Porthmadog for a whole month, and it would be easier to think that there is a gap in the coverage given in the Shipping Intelligence columns located.

The snapshots continue with arrival at Porthdinllaen on 24 May (*North Wales Chronicle*, 27 May, 1854), sailing from Caernarfon on 27 July (*North Wales Chronicle*, 29 July 1854), arrival at Porthdinllaen on 19 October (*North Wales Chronicle*, 21 October 1854), and sailing from Porthdinllaen on 2 November (*North Wales Chronicle*, 4 November 1854).

The Shipping Intelligence columns of 1855 give the following snapshots: 1 March, sailed from Porthdinllaen (*North Wales Chronicle*, 3 March), 8 March, sailed from Porthdinllaen (*North Wales Chronicle*, 10 March). This would suggest a very short voyage in the meantine, to be back there in a week.

The next report found, in the *North Wales Chronicle* of 19 May, is of a sailing from Porthdinllaen, followed by another sailing from the same port on 31 May (*North Wales Chronicle* of 2 June).

On 7 July, the *North Wales Chronicle's* Shipping Intelligence column reports that the Ellen and Ann arrived at Porthdinllaen on 5 July.

The next reference found is in the Shipping Intelligence of a South Wales newspaper, *The Welshman*, on 20 July, which reports the *Ellen and Ann* arriving at Carmarthen from Caernarfon with slates, and then sailingfrom Carmarthen.

On 9 August the *Ellen and Ann* arrived at Porthdinllaen, and sailed from there the same day (*North Wales Chronicle,* 11 August 1855), and on 5 September again sailed sailed from Porthdinllaen (*North Wales Chronicle*, 8 September 1855), and arrived at the same port on 11 October (*North Wales Chronicle*, 13 October 1855), and also sailed from there on 13 December (*North Wales Chronicle*, 15 December 1855).

The next chapter describes his career on the *Eleanor and Jane*, a ship in which he owned 54 shares out of 64, and the other shares were allocated four each to his father and his widowed sister Sydney Evans, and two to David Rice Hughes, sailmaker of Porthdinllaen, and a very successful investor in ships. This tragically ended with John getting into financial difficulties and having to sell all his shares to David Rice Hughes, but at least the combination of the crew lists and ledgers paint a very detailed picture of the voyages and the transactions involved.

The Eleanor and Jane

The *Eleanor and Jane* was built on 23 January 1856 at Porthdinllaen by H Hughes, and weighed 89 tons, was 67.6 feet long, 21 feet broad, and 10.9 feet deep, with a square stern, carvel build (i.e. having the plank flush at the edges, opposite of clinker built), two masts, one deck and had a female bust as head stem. Register Number 14,929. It would seem that the ship was named after John's mother Eleanor, and his wife Jane.

On 12 April 1856 John was registered as the owner of 54 shares, while the remaining shares were four held by his father, William Griffiths, a retired mariner, and four held by his widowed sister Sydney Evans, and two held by David Rice Hughes, sail maker of Porthdinllaen. It was the custom for ships to be divided into 64 shares, and this was made law by an act in 1825. John still lived at Cwmistir Bach, but by 1858 he lived at Llain Fadryn.

The very patchy nature of the run of Shipping Intelligence reports avilable on Welsh Newspapers Online is shown by the fact that I have only traced one reference to the *Eleanor and Jane* in each of the years 1856 and 1857. This may be due to gaps in the runs of the *North Wales Chronicle* and *Carnarvon and Denbigh Herald* at the National Library of Wales, or that the Optical Character Recognition software used in transcribing the reports might be distorting the search terms, so as to miss some relevant entries. Certainly, any ports outside of Wales will fall outside the remit of the columns consulted.

The 1856 entry refers to the *Eleanor and Jane* arriving at Caernarfon on 30 October (*North Wales Chronicle*, 1 November 1856), while the 1857 reference is to sailing from Caernarfon on 17 September (*North Wales Chronicle*, 19 September 1857). It can be safely assumed that the *Eleanor and Jane* would not have stayed in port for almost a year.

No Shipping Intelligence report has been found for the *Eleanor and Jane* in 1858, but in June 1858 John Griffiths mislaid his master's certificate in Limerick, Ireland, while he was on shore, transacting business for the ship, but did not know in what manner he lost or mislaid it. On 27 April 1859 he declared to James Walters, one of the Justices of the Peace of the Borough of Swansea, that he had mislaid his certificate. Three days later he was issued with his new certificate, number 72,521, at Swansea.

The Shipping Intelligence column of 12 February 1859 records that on 10 February the *Eleanor and Jane* arrived at Porthdinllaen.

The 1860 references are to the *Eleanor and Jane* arriving at Porthmadog from Dublin on 15 November (*North Wales Chronicle*, 17 November 1860), and sailing from Porthmadog to Sunderland on 13 December (*North Wales Chronicle*, 15 December 1860).

The Lloyds register of Master Mariners at the Guildhall Library in London fills in some of the voyages of the *Eleanor and Jane* for the early 1860s, but it is with the crew lists in Gwynedd Archives, Caernarfon from 1863 onwards that we start having details of ports of call apart from the incidental mentions of Limerick and Swansea above. The code for the voyages are Ct, meaning coasting in the British Isles and the continent from Brest to the Elbe, and FPS, meaning France south of Brest, Portugal, and Spain outside the Straits of Gibraltar.

He was on the *Eleanor and Jane* from 11 March to 12 June 1861, and was not at home at the time of the census, although his wife lived at Ty Newydd, next door to Llain Madryn at the time. His voyages during both halves of 1862 are similarly noted without any details.

The Shipping Intelligence reports for 1861 help to throw some light on the movements of the *Eleanor and Jane* beyond the vague information of the Lloyds register of Master Mariners. The *North Wales Chronicle* of 23 March refers to *Eleanor and Jane* sailing from Porthdinllaen to Port Nant.

Port Nant is more familiar to us today as Nant Gwrtheyrn, now a Welsh language teaching centre, but was then a granite quarrying village. Granite setts were much in demand in the 1850s and 1860s for cobblestones for the rapidly growing cities such as Manchester, Liverpool and Birkenhead. Hugh Owen from Anglesey, in 1851, was the first to attempt to open a granite quarry at Nant Gwrtheyrn. In 1861 a Liverpool-based company, Kneeshaw and Lupton opened a quarry on the southern side of the bay. Thes was an ideal site for the quarry as there was a large supply of granite nearby, and is also close to the sea. It is also not very far from Nefyn and Porthdinllaen.

On 15 June 1861 the *North Wales Chronicle* referred to the *Eleanor and Jane* clearing out of Port Penrhyn, Bangor, with slates.

On 14 December 1861 the *Cardiff and Merthyr Guardian* refers to the *Eleanor and Jane* sailing from the West Bute docks in Cardiff on the Monday, bound for Liverpool with a cargo of coal. The West Bute Docks, opened in 1839, and the East Bute Docks, opened in 1855, were created by the 2nd Marquess of Bute, a prominent landowner in the area, to take advantage of the opportunities presented by Cardiff being a foremost centre of the iron and coal industries.

Illustration 2: The Bute Docks in Cardiff as seen in 1853

The *North Wales Chronicle*'s Shipping Intelligence columns in 1862 refers to arriving at Porthmadog on 24 April from Dublin (26 April), and sailing from Porthmadog on 29 May to London (29 May).

In January to June 1863 we find the first crew list returns available in Caernarfon Record office.

The *Eleanor and Jane* sailed from Swansea to Corunna and ports in Spain, Portugal, France and back to a final port of discharge in the United Kingdom. The crew consisted of Robert Owen of Llanarmon,

William Evans of Nefyn, Ellis Jones of Pwllheli, who had previously served on the *Eliza* of Pwllheli, and John Phillips of Cardigan, who had previously served in the *Carrie* of Wexford, Ireland. The crews of John Griffiths's ship tended usually to be mostly Welsh, and especially from Nefyn, Pwllheli and Porthmadog. 236 seems to be the *Eleanor and Jane*'s rotation number at Swansea.

Although this crew list does not list all the movements of the ship on this voyage, the *North Wales Chronicle* of 23 May, mentions that the *Eleanor and Jane* departed from Porthdinllaen to Barmouth on 21 May.

During the second half of 1863 the crew consisted of John himself, Thomas Richard, John Williams, William Edwards and Ellis Williams, and all, apart from Thomas Richard, had previously served on the *Eleanor and Jane*. The voyage was to Corunna and back to Liverpool, where all accounts were deposited, and then on to the River Dee. Corunna was a fishing port, and the Galician coast is famous for shellfish and crustaceans, but it may be doubted if those would keep fresh on a long sea voyage. Further details given are that on 23 June to 21 September, she sailed from Swansea to Spain, and 5 October-31 December sailed to Spain. On 5 October 1863 the *Eleanor and Jane* left Liverpool for Queensferry, and arrived there 6 October. On 19 October 1863 she left Queensferry for London, but on 3 December was stranded on Nefyn beach for repairs.

On 29 December 1863 we can see an early indication of possible financial problems as John mortgaged his 54 shares in the Eleanor and Jane to David Rice Hughes, at £500 at 5% per annum. This mortgage was apparently discharged in 1867.

From 30 May to 20 August 1864 he sailed from Cardiff to Ipswich, but the details given suggests that on 30 May the voyage was from Cardiff to Gibraltar, and on 20 August, to Gibraltar.

On 12 September 1864, however, there is no ambiguity in the records. The *Eleanor and Jane* left Ipswich carrying coprolites (a kind of fossilised dung used as fertiliser) to Plymouth. This is the first time in the crew lists that the actual cargo is described. The *Eleanor and Jane* and her cargo arrived at Plymouth on 20 October 1864.

On 28 October 1864 she left Plymouth with ballast for Par, near the Cornish clay mines, in order to pick up clay for Runcorn, and on 28 November arrived at Runcorn.

On 30 November the *Eleanor and Jane* left Runcorn with salt for Ostend, and arrived there on 3 January 1865. Runcorn was an industrialised area, and also very near to the Cheshire salt mines.

On 19 January 1865 she left Ostend carrying ballast to Ipswich, where she arrived on 25 January. Sadly the cargo is not mentioned on subsequent crew lists, but it can be safely assumed that slates from Caernarfon, coal from Newcastle and South Wales, and china clay from Cornwall, manufactured goods from Liverpool, and agricultural produce from Llyn would play a fairly important role in the ship's trade. They were certainly the cargoes on other similar ships of the time.

On 6 April 1865 she sailed from Cardiff to Seville and on 29 June from Seville to Shields. The voyage from 21 Sep 1865 to 31 Dec 1865 is not detailed at all. It may be that coal may have been the cargo on this voyage. The *Eleanor and Jane* was certainly at West Bute Docks, Cardiff on December 14, 1865.

On 14 April 1866 the crew agreement details the voyage to be undertaken as "To Lisbon, and if agreed, Corunna and Pomano (Pomarao) or any port or ports as freight or employment may offer for the ship and until her return at a final port of discharge in the United Kingdom. Term of service shall not exceed 12 months". Pomarao is a small port on the Portuguese side of the Guadiana River, and from 1859 onwards the company that owned the São Domingos Mines built a settlement with warehouses, railway and docks. The arrangement was that the railway would transport the ore (pyrites) from the mines to the port, for loading onto ships. With a draft of 12 feet, this was the highest point at which the Guadiana is navigable. In 1864, 563 ships called at Pomarao to collect ore, so this was a fairly busy small port.

Illustration 3: Ship loading pyrites at the dock in the Portuguese mining port of Pomarao

The *North Wales Chronicle* of April 28, 1866 records the *Eleanor and Jane* arriving at Porthdinllaen from Greenock, which is certainly not en route to and from Lisbon.

Provisions were usually specified as being "sufficient without waste" or where detailed would be: Beef (1.5 lb issued on Sunday, Monday, Wednesday, Thursday and Saturday), Bread (1lb daily), Flour (1.5lbs on Sunday and Thursday), Pork (1.5lbs on Tuesday and Friday), Tea (1.75 oz weekly), Coffee (3.5 oz weekly), Sugar (14 oz weekly), Water (3 quarts daily), and substitutes may be given for any or all of these provisions at a proportionate rate.

In June 1866 the *Eleanor and Jane* sailed from "Newcastle to Huelva, and if agreed, to any other port or ports, place or places in Spain, Portugal and France and back to any port or ports in the United Kingdom"

The stages that are detailed in other sources are: 16 July 1866 voyage Newcastle to Lisbon, 28 October 1866 arrived in Huelva, 15 December Huelva to Newcastle. Huelva in southern Spain is near the Rio Tinto, which is a rich copper-producing area, so this may be a possible cargo, although corkwood, pyrites and sulphur ore are other products of this area.

On 1 January 1867 was at Newcastle the *Eleanor and Jane* was involved in the coasting trade between any ports in the United Kingdom and the continent of Europe.

On 26 January she left Newcastle for Poole. On 7 March she left Poole for Glasgow and on 4 May she left Glasgow for Dieppe. On first sight it would seem as if this was a straightforward voyage from Glasgow to Dieppe, especially as the next voyage listed in the log book, is from Dieppe to Runcorn on 10 June, but the *North Wales Chronicle* suggests that the itinerary was much more complicated, with the 30 March report of the *Eleanor and Jane* arriving at Porthdinllaen from Poole, and on 18 May, arriving at Porthdinllaen from Glasgow. Depending on the log books and crew lists alone can present a misleadingly straightforward picture.

On 10 June she left Dieppe for Runcorn, but was apparently still at sea on 30 June if we believe log book without question. The Carnarvon and Denbigh Herald of 1867 shows that she arrived at Porthdinllaen, which would be on the likely route. It would seem that the log books don't list all the ports visited.

On 15 July the log book for the first half of 1867 was deposited at Runcorn. The crew which included William Ellis, Richard Freeman, Robert Herd and Edward Parry were all marked in the log book as being "very good" both in general conduct and in their ability as seamen. Although the logbook mentions the voyages Glasgow-Dieppe and Dieppe-Runcorn, there are no details of anything occurring on these voyages. Subsequent logbooks also, without any exceptions, seem to depict rather uneventful voyages without any deviations from "very good" for the crew.

On 20 July she left Runcorn and arrived at Pwllheli on 26 July. The *North Wales Chronicle* for 3 August 1867, adds that the *Eleanor and Jane* arrived at Porthdinllaen, and then sailed to Pwllheli.

On 21 August, at 10am, John Griffith bought David Rice Hughes's two shares, so he was clearly at home at that date.

On 12 September John sailed from Pwllheli and on 13 September arrived at Porthmadog. The *North Wales Chronicle* of September 21, also has the *Eleanor and Jane* arriving at Porthmadog from Pwllheli.

On 26 September the mortgage on John's 54 shares was discharged, so the situation until 14 December 1871 was that John held 56 shares, his father 4 and his sister 4. That day John also sailed from Porthmadog to London, where he arrived on 10 October. Yet the *North Wales Chronicle* of 5 October 1867, also mentions the *Eleanor and Jane* sailing from Porthmadog, presumably just a few days before the date of the newspaper report, so the true date of the sailing is probably in the first few days of October.

On 20 October he sailed from London to Bristol, where he arrived on 12 November. On 22 November he left Bristol, and arrived at Cardiff on 23 November.

On 10 December the *Eleanor and Jane* left Cardiff for Dublin, and arrived there on 20 December. On 29 December she left Dublin for Bristol, but arrived there on 29 January 1868, probably due to adverse winds, and John had to explain why he was late with his returns.

He left Bristol on 27 February, and arrived at Neath on 27 March. On 30 March the *Eleanor and Jane* left Neath, and arrived at Drogheda, Ireland on 4 April. On 10 April she left Drogheda, and arrived at Caernarfon on 14 April. On 18 April she left Caernarfon, and arrived at London 21 April. It seems as if the length of voyages depends on the weather, as it seems inconceivable that it would take a month to go from Bristol to Neath, and yet a mere three days for the more complex one from Caernarfon to London.

On 24 April the *Eleanor and Jane* left London, and arrived at Newhaven 29 April. On 3 May she left Newhaven and arrived at Runcorn on 8 May. On 12 May she left Runcorn and arrived at Caernarfon on 30 June. Again it seems that a relatively short journey has taken a long time.

On 2 July the *Eleanor and Jane* left Caernarfon, and arrived at London on 4 July 1868. The log said that the delivery of the return had been delayed by contrary winds. This would seem to refer to the Runcorn to Caernarfon leg of the journey, since the Caernarfon to London run did not take an inordinately long time.

On 10 July the *Eleanor and Jane* left Newhaven, but the crew list has not mentioned the voyage from London to Newhaven, which undoubtedly must have taken place. She arrived at Runcorn on 2 August. On 14 August she left Runcorn and arrived at Newry on 30 August. On 12 September she left Newry and arrived at London on 23 October. She left London on 1 November and arrived at Swansea on 23 November. On 16 December she left Swansea and arrived at Llanaelhaearn on 21 December.

The shipping intelligence columns in the North Wales newspapers again show that the true picture is rather more complex than the above account of the second half of 1868, with a sailing from Porthdinllaen to Newry (*North Wales Chronicle*, 25 July); sailing from Porthdinllaen (*Carnarvon and Denbigh Herald*, 1 August); arrival at Porthdinllaen from Llanaelhaearn (*North Wales Chronicle*, 10 October). It seems that reconstructing the itinerary of a voyage is like a jigsaw, where crew lists, log books and newspaper reports all contribute towards building up the picture.

From the 1 January 1869 to 10 March the *Eleanor and Jane* was being repaired if we go by the log book, but the *Carnarvon and Denbigh Herald* of 9 January refers to her sailing from Porthdinllaen. (It is possible that this voyage is to the place where she was to be repaired)

On 10 March she left Caernarfon for London, and on 8 March left London for Whitehaven. On 10 May she left Whitehaven for Rouen, and on 30 May left Rouen for Garston, near Liverpool. On 28 June she left Garston for Runcorn. The *North Wales Chronicle* of June 26 adds that she sailed from Porthdinllaen to Garston, so clearly one of the last stages on this voyage.

On 8 July she left Runcorn for "Dardt", almost certainly Dordrecht (Dort) in Holland. On 17 August she left Dardt, for Barrow, and on 1 October left Barrow for Rotterdam.

Illustration 4: Dordrecht around 1900, from a Photocrom print at the Library of Congress

On 1 November she left Rotterdam for Barrow, and deposited the logbook on 20 January 1870.

On 10 February she left Barrow, and arrived at Swansea on 17 February. On 4 March she left Swansea, and arrived at Cork on 7 March. On 31 March she left Cork and arrived at Garston on 10 April, and left Garston 6 May, and on 9 May arrived at Maryport (probably the Cumbria one rather than the smaller Galloway one). She left Maryport on 22 May and arrived at Calais. On 13 June she left Calais and arrived at Middlesbrough on 22 June. She left Middlesbrough on 29 June and arrived at Swansea on 13 July. She left Swansea on 23 July and arrived at Dieppe on 25 August. On 29 August she left Dieppe and arrived at Runcorn on 6 September.

On 20 September the *Eleanor and Jane* left Runcorn, and arrived at Charleston on 30 September (This is probably Charlestown in Cornwall). She left Charleston on 2 October, and arrived at Runcorn on 14 October. On 26 November she left Runcorn, and arrived at Dublin on 27 November. On 30 November she left Dublin and arrived 2 December at Llanaelhaearn, a quarry port not very far from Nefyn. She left Llanaelhaearn on 26 December and arrived at London on 10 January 1871.

During January to June 1871 she sailed from London to Amlwch, then to Llanaelhaearn, Liverpool, Amlwch and Belfast. The register of service records a voyage from 12 March to 11 July 1871, without any details of ports, but it may reasonably be thought they were those listed for January to June. John's address was given as Cwmistir.

The sole Shipping Intelligence reference to the *Eleanor and Jane* in 1871 presents a surprise, which might be a clue that things were not exactly as they should be. The *North Wales Chronicle* of 6 May 1871, mentions a voyage of the *Eleanor and Jane* from Holyhead to Valentio (presumably Valencia, Spain, unless anybody can suggest a more likely destination), but the captain named in this reference is Davies! The crew lists and log books consulted give no hint of this.

On 20 July 1871 the *Eleanor and Jane* left Belfast, and arrived at Barrow on 31 July. She left Barrow on 26 August, and arrived at Liverpool on 31 August, left Liverpool on 2 September, and arrived at Barrow on 10 September. She left Barrow on 20 October, and arrived at Swansea on 23 October, left Swansea on 29 October, and arrived at Porthdinllaen on 31 October. The following day John and all his crew left the ship, apart from Elias Williams the new captain and controlling owner of the ship. The next chapter examines the events which led to this change of ownership.

John Griffiths's Financial Difficulties

David Rice Hughes, the sailmaker, who held two shares in the *Eleanor and Jane*, was also the "ship's husband", the man ashore who looked after the accounts for the ship, and kept the ship's registration up to date, and often was accountable for the ship's profitable operation..

He was born in Pwllheli in 1827, and in the 1850s he came to Bwlch, Morfa Nefyn, where he set up business as a sail maker. However he soon realised that diversifying into dealing in imported merchandise such as lime (used as a fertiliser for the acidic soil of Llŷn), coal (used as a domestic fuel) and culm (used as an industrial fuel). He also owned shares in many ships, such as the *Eleanor and Jane*, and if a ship owner owed him a considerable amount of money he would effect a mortgage on that ship, usually at an interest rate of 6%. As we have already seen this was done on the *Eleanor and Jane*, but other examples are the *Miss Pritchard* owned by John Pritchard, and the *Pamela Pennant*, owned by Richard Griffiths.

Rice Hughes's ledgers record such outgoings as insurance payments to Thomas and Garrett, and the Nevin insurance club, and payments to ships' carpenters for repairs to the ship, supplies of coal tar and canvas, and receipts of money, undoubtedly sent by post from some of the ports where the *Eleanor and Jane* called, e.g. on 13 August 1868 remittance of £15 from London and on 9 June £20 from Rouen. Most of the entries in any ledgers are rather mundane, but there are clues that John's financial situation was not as healthy as it may be. In the 1869 accounts there is on 17 September (1868) a mention of "By arrears debit mortgage on *Eleanor and Jane* £1 18/11.5d" which is not to be expected if the mortgage was discharged on 26 September 1867, and on 15 September 1869 To 12 months interest on £432 12/1.5 at rate 6% £25 15/6.

Clearly the shares transaction register in Caernarfon must be presenting a rather simplified picture of the financial situation, which is not the true one.

Another significant sign of difficulties is the occurrence of a number of advances of small sums of money to John Griffiths. Examples are:

10 November (1868). To cash allowance to John Griffith   £5
30 Nov. (1869) To cash advance to John Griffith.   11/-
10 May. (1870). To carry advance to John Griffith Per OUH   £5
2 June. To cash advance to John Griffith   £10.
12 July. -13/ To cash advance to John Griffith per OUH.
12 July.   73 400 to 24 months interest on £12 at 5% per annum   £1 4/-

All these imply that John had got into financial difficulties, and the family legend says that he was rather too fond of drink. His son William was a total abstainer, probably as a result of the influence of his mother and maternal grandparents, who were staunch Calvinistic Methodists, but certainly the example of his father served as a cautionary tale on the impoverishing effects of alcohol.

Although John left the *Eleanor and Jane* on 1 November 1871, when Elias Williams became the new controlling owner, the official records of share transactions seem to lag behind the reality of the situation.

John's father William had died intestate on 21 February 1871, and his daughter Sydney Evans was not granted letters of administration until 11 December. She inherited her father's four shares, so she now held eight shares, which she sold soon after John sold his 56 shares to David Rice Hughes on 14 December. This begs the question of why the legal situation lagged behind the de facto situation by a month and a half.

While John's drinking would certainly have contributed to his difficulties, it must also be said that the coming of the railways would have meant that there was an alternative means of transport for some of the coasting journeys, although the 1870s was generally a very prosperous time for the Caernarfonshire slate quarries, and therefore for the ships that transported the slates. The really successful shipping companies were those like the Davieses of Treborth, Bangor, who had large ocean-going ships which went to Canada and South America. By the standards of the 1870s the Eleanor and Jane was a very small ship.

By 1879 the *Eleanor and Jane* was owned by Robert Williams of Nefyn. She was abandoned on 29 November 1887 off Loch Broome in Scotland.

John's subsequent career is rather difficult to reconstruct, after the quite detailed records on the *Eleanor and Jane*. He appears in the Lloyd's Captains Register as sailing in 1873 on the *Mary Lawson* (official number 44,527) of Chester, a 140 ton brigantine built at Pallion, owned by James Reney of Connah's Quay. On 20 June 1873 he sailed from Chester to Santander in northern Spain, and sailed back from there on 1 August. The Lloyds Captains register does not give any further voyages for John Griffiths. The *Mary Lawson* was lost on 14 April 1874, blown ashore by a gale at San Sebastian, Spain, with the loss of two lives. The report in the *Cambrian News and Merionethshire* Standard of 8 May, 1874, the *Manchester Courier and Lancashire General Advertiser*, (and several other regional newspapers) gives an account of this tragedy where the lives of two crewmen and a customs officer were lost, but the master, mate and one crewman were saved. This report is by a correspondent at San Sebastian, and does not actually name the people aboard, so we cannot be 100% sure that John Griffiths is the master referred to:

LOSS OF A CHESTER SCHOONER AND THREE LIVES: A correspondent at San Sebastian writes "On the 14th ult the English schooner *Mary Lawson*, of Chester with a cargo of coal for Bayonne, drove from her mooriongs under the lee of the little island of Santa Clara, which forms a sort of breakwater at the entrance of the bay, and drove upon the sands, which from their fineness, compactness and gradual decline, have made San Sebastian the principal bathing place in Spain. A lifeboat could have saved the whole crew esily, but the one belonging to this port had been laid up so long in some corner on shore as to have become useless. No attempt, however, was made to prove her seaworthiness so out of a crew of five individuals two seamen perished,together with the ill-fated douanier, or carabiniero, who had been put on board to prevent smuggling.

Illustration 5: The harbour at San Sebastian, Spain, scene of the loss of the Mary Lawson

John appeared in the 1881 census at Llain Madryn, Morfa Nefyn, as a mariner, but in around 1886 he moved to Liverpool, when his granddaughter Ann (born 1882) was four years old.

He certainly lived at 82 Highfield Street in 1889, and died there on 17 March 1890. He left all his estate to his wife, who proved his will, and the estate amounted to £29 10/-, which does not seem to be much for someone who once owned almost a whole ship, worth over £500. He was buried at Edern Calvinistic Methodist church, near Morfa Nefyn, and his wife Jane later came back to Nefyn to live with her daughter, and died in 1905.

William Griffiths (1865-1959): Part 1: 1880s.

The maritime career of the William Griffiths born in 1865 was actually made very easy to trace. In most cases trying to reconstruct the career of a mariner can involve starting with the crew list for his most recent known voyage, which will also name his previous ship, and then working backwards.

The crew lists might be in the Records offices covering the port of registration of the ship, but many are kept at the Public Records Office in Kew, London, and it is said that 70% of surviving crew lists have been transferred to the Memorial University of Newfoundland, in Canada. The potential cost of following a paper trail which could involve London, Liverpool, Glasgow, Cardiff and Canada could be quite daunting.

In this particular case a rather complete run of his discharge papers had passed down to his grand-daughter, the late Mrs Eurwen Bradbury, of Pensarn, near Amlwch, and was deposited at the Gwynedd County Archives in Caernarfon.

Moreover, many of these ships were registered at Caernarfon and Beaumaris, so the crew lists for these ships were accessible locally at Caernarfon and Llangefni, so the full details of the voyages on the *Venerable*, *Hugh Roberts*, the *Ocean Wave* and the Penrhyn Quarries ship the *Harrier*, can be found easily. It must be said that almost all his early ships had local connections, including the Glasgow-registered *Saigon*, whose managing owner lived at Nefyn.

The wealth of information that can be gleaned from the discharge papers, crew lists and other documents is enough to justify dealing with William's life in three chapters.

William appears in the 1881 census at Llain Madryn, Nefyn, aged 16 and is described as a mariner.

On 14 September 1882, at Portdinorwic, he entered service on the *Venerable*, official number 4,148 of Caernarfon, tonnage 86. The *Venerable* was a schooner built at Borthwen, Merioneth in 1844. He was an Ordinary Seaman in the coasting trade. He was previously on the *J N Smith* of Liverpool. The discharge paper gives his date of entry as 13 September. David Parry, aged 40, born at Nefyn and previously on the *Rebecca* of Caernarfon also joined on September 14. The master was William Jones, aged 46, and a native of Barmouth. On 18 September the *Venerable* sailed from Portdinorwic to Torquay, and arrived there 23 September. On 3 October she left Torquay for Caernarfon, and arrived at Caernarfon on 16 October.

The managing owner of the *Venerable* was Rees Jones, of Port Dinorwic, who had started as a shipbuilder in the Barmouth area, and gained the reputation of the best shipbuilder in Gwynedd. He later moved to Portdinorwic as a result of an invitation by the Methodists in the area who were impressed by his preaching.

William was discharged from the *Venerable* at Caernarfon, and was described as good for both conduct and ability, on the Register of Shipping and Seamen certificate, but very good for both on his discharge paper. His discharge paper was signed by William Jones, the master, and witnessed by Robert Owen of the Harbour Office, Caernarfon, ship agent.

On 12 January 1883 he joined the *Saigon*, official number 59,988 of Glasgow with a registered tonnage of 767. She had no horsepower to the engines, which presumably meant she was purely a sailing ship. The *Saigon* was a barque built in Quebec in 1871, and its managing owner was William Thomas of Tyn y Coed, Nefyn, who was also prominent in the Pwllheli and Nefyn ship insuring club. William was then 18 and described as Ordinary Seaman. The master was William Davies. The voyage was to Huanillos in Chile, which was one of the ports where guano was loaded. Such a distant port would mean a long voyage, and on 10 January 1884 he was discharged at London and described as very good for both conduct and ability.

Although the discharge paper puts his voyage as being to Huanillos, the *South Wales Daily News* of 15 January 1883, paints a slightly fuller picture, in that the *Saigon* cleared from West Bute Dock, Cardiff on 13 January, with a cargo of coals for Montevideo, in Uruguay, which would be conveniently on the route to Chile.

The final leg of the voyage is also recorded by the *South Wales Daily* news of 8 January 1884, where it is mentioned that the *Saigon* of Glasgow was signalled at the Lizard signalling station, on her route from Queenstown to London. Queenstown is the Irish port of Cobh, county Cork, which was renamed Queenstown in 1849 after the visit of Queen Victoria, and reverted to its old name in the early 1920s, under the Irish Free State.

On 22 March he was again engaged on the *Saigon*, at Swansea, and the voyage is described as "Foreign", without specifying the destination, and was discharged at Dunkirk on 30 November 1885, which suggests that this was another very long voyage, and was again described as very good.

Reports in newspapers actually fill in a lot of the details of this voyage, and show that this voyage was to South America, and was not without incident . The *South Wales Daily News* of March 24, 1884 shows that the Saigon left Swansea on March 22 with a cargo of coal for Buenos Aires.

The spontaneous combustion of flammable cargoes, such as guano or coal, was an occupational hazard of a life at sea, and all the more serious if the ship was built of timber. The *Weekly Mail* of November 22, 1884 has the account of the *Saigon* rescuing the crew of a Swansea-based ship which caught fire in such circumstances:

"ABANDONMENT OF A SWANSEA BARQUENTINE. SUPPOSED CASE OF SPONTANEOUS COMBUSTION. The Press Association has received a copy of the findings of a Naval Court of Inquiry held at the British Consulate, Valparaiso, in the abandonment of the barquentine *Bridegroom* of Swansea on the 3rd of September last. The Court arrived at the following decision "That the *Bridegroom*, a wooden vessel of 497 tons or thereabout, belonging to the port of Swansea (official number 71,430), which sailed from Garson on the 7th day of June last, laden with a cargo of steam coal, bound for Valparaiso, was found on fire on the 3rd instant and was abandoned in or about latitude 45 south and longitude 78 west; that at the time of the abandonment the cargo showed signs of being in a rapidly burning condition; that the barque *Saigon*, of Glasgow, having gone to their assistance, the master and crew of the *Bridegroom* were justified in abandoning that vessel and taking refuge on board the *Saigon* without delay; that the fire originated from spontaneous combustion of the cargo of coals and from no other cause, and there is no appearance of any illegal or wrongful act on the part of the master of the Bridegroom, and the Court, attaching no blame to them, has pleasure in returning to Mr Charles Stephens, the master, and to Mr Charles Frederick, the mate, their certificates."

On 6 February 1886 he was engaged on the *Hugh Roberts*, official number 70,310 of Caernarfon, 180 tons, which had been built in Porthmadog in 1876. This ship was involved in the coasting trade to Hamburg. William was an Able Seaman. His previous ship was the *Saigon* of Glasgow. The period of service was not to exceed 6 months. The captain was John Jones of Caernarfon.

The managing owner was Hugh Roberts, ship broker of Quayside, Newcastle, who was the son of Bryn Gwydd Farm, Edern, and a former schooner captain. Hugh Roberts had been running a steam ship business in partnership with Edward Beck, a slate merchant of Newcastle, but by 1875 he was running the business on his own account, and in 1877 invested in his first iron screw steamer. His company was very successful and survived both world wars.

The crew who joined on 6 February were William Williams, Frederick Jones, Daniel Jones, Charles Jones, William Griffiths, William Roberts, and Evan Hughes.

On 9 February Thomas Jones joined at Bangor.

On 5 March the *Hugh Roberts* arrived at Cuxham, an out port of Hamburg, and the agreement was deposited there on 8 March and returned on 17 March.

On 12 April the *Hugh Roberts* arrived at Hamburg, and the articles were deposited there the same day, and returned on 15 April. On 17 April the *Hugh Roberts* was at the Elbe, where William Williams joined the crew.

These early ships had connections with Nefyn, through the captain in the case of the *Venerable*, and the owners in the case of the *Saigon* and *Hugh Roberts*, and no doubt he would have known many of the other crew, since many were also from the Nefyn and Edern area.

William Griffiths was discharged from the *Hugh Roberts* on 30 April. It seems that his next ship was the *Jane Gwynne*, a schooner, official number 21,751 of Aberystwyth. She was built at Aberdyfi in 1858, and was 87 tons, and belonged to John Lewis of Rock Terrace, Barmouth. Although William's discharge paper for the *Jane Gwynne* is not extant, this was the ship he quoted as his previous ship when he joined the *Ocean Wave* on 31 July. We can therefore date the voyage on the *Jane Gwynne* as being sometime during May, June or July.

On 31 July, at Caernarfon, he joined the *Ocean Wave*, official number 74,869 of Caernarfon, 157 tons, and involved in the foreign trade. The master of the *Ocean Wave* was Cobden Evans. The Ocean Wave had been built in Cosheston, Pembrokeshire in 1876.

The agreement described the voyage as being from Caernarfon to Trieste and thence to any ports wherever freights may offer in the Mediterranean, Spain, Portugal, North or South America, East or West Indies, Brazils, North Atlantic or United States, Gulf of Mexico, Coast of Morocco, Sweden or Norway and back to a final port of discharge in the United Kingdom or the Continent of Europe, term not to exceed 18 months. The description of the possible destinations seems to exclude only most of Africa, the Far East, and Australia and New Zealand.

The managing owner of the *Ocean Wave* was Meyrick Ellis of Portdinorwic.

The ship had accommodation for nine seamen.

The provisions were detailed as Bread: 1 lb on all days: Beef, 1.5 lbs on Sunday, Tuesday, Thursday and Saturday; Pork, 1.25 lbs on Monday, Wednesday, and Friday; flour, 0.5 lb on 4 days a week, Peas 0.3pt on Mon, Wed and Fri; Rice 1 lb weekly; Coffee 0.5 oz daily; tea 0.125z daily, water 3 quarts daily

The crew were listed as follows:

Cobden Evans, Captain born 1860 at Pwllheli.

The rest of the crew joined on July 31 1886 at Caernarfon.

Robert Pritchard, Mate, born 1848 at Nevin, formerly of the *CE Spooner* of Caernarfon. Discharged September 17 1887 at Porthmadog.

William Griffith formerly on *Jane Gwynne* of Aberystwyth, AB, discharged 12 September 1887 at Dublin. Balance of wages £32 12/11

Hugh Hughes born 1865 at Nefyn, formerly on the *Elizabeth Thomas* of Aberystwyth, discharged 17 September 1887 at Porthmadog.

Owen Roberts, born 1868 at Pwllheli, first voyage. Ordinary Seaman and cook, discharged September 17 1887 at Porthmadog.

Henry Lewis, born 1863 at Gloucester, formerly of *Ocean Shield* of Caernarfon. AB, Discharged at Porthmadog on September 17 1887.

On 28 1886 September the *Ocean Wave* arrived at Trieste, which is now in Italy, but was then part of the Austrian empire until after the First World War, and the articles were deposited the same day. The articles were returned on 16 October.

Illustration 6: Trieste in 1885, now in Italy, but was then a port of the Austrian Empire

On 16 February 1887 she arrived at Rio de Janeiro, Brazil, and her articles were deposited on the 17th and returned on the 18th.

On Saturday 12 March 1887 the *Ocean Wave* arrived at Rio Grande do Sul, Brazil, and the articles were deposited on 14 March and returned on the 29th.

On 28 July she was at Hamburg, Germany, and the articles were deposited on 31 July and returned 23 August.

William was discharged from the *Ocean Wave* at Dublin on 12 September, and on the 13th the log is stamped and returned. The crew are said to be willing to be discharged at Portdinorwic. The voyage terminated at Portdinorwic, and William is described as good for conduct, but declined on ability. This seems the only less than glowing report he had, when on his other voyages he is assessed as very good.

On 28 February 1888 he joined the *Antofagasta* of Liverpool as an able seaman. The *Antofagasta*, official number 70,935 of Liverpool, of 678 tons (a sailing ship built in Sunderland 1875), was engaged in the foreign trade. On 22 December he was discharged from the *Antofagasta*, and was described as very good for both conduct and ability.

No reports were found in the Shipping Intelligence columns of voyages of the *Ocean Wave*. The South Wales newspapers do have references to voyages by a ship called the *Ocean Wave*, which was, quite understandably a popular name for ships at the time, but this was one of 139 tons, which tallies with the Appledore registered ship of that name. The South Wales newspapers of the time helpfully gave the tonnage of the ships, which helps with identification.

On 1 January 1889 (but 25 December 1888 according to his discharge paper) he entered the *Princess Alice* as an Able Seaman. The *Princess Alice*, official number 53,405 of Glasgow, 353 tons, 130 horsepower, was involved in the coasting trade.

The shipping intelligence columns of the *South Wales Daily News* give the distinct impression that the *Princess Alice's* voyages are mainly between South Wales and Scotland. The 29 December 1888 edition mentions the *Princess Alice* (353 tons) arriving at West Bute Dock, Cardiff on 27 December, and on 28 December at East Bute Dock with sundries from Dundee. On 28 December she sailed, under Captain Sinclair, for Aberdeen.

The *South Wales Daily News* of 23 January 1889 shows that this must have been a very regular voyage, since on 22 January the *Princess Alice* (353) tons arrived at East Bute Dock, Cardiff, with sundries from Dundee, and the edition of 24 January mentions her sailing under Captain Sinclair for Aberdeen. He was discharged from the *Princess Alice* on 4 March. He was described as Very Good for both conduct and ability. The master was L Sinclair and the witness was Donald Munro of 65 Lumsden St, Glasgow, 2nd Mate.

On 9 April he was engaged on the *Tuskar,* official number 47,817 of Glasgow, 287 tons. 70 horse power, and involved in the coasting trade (Code given as HINK). Built in Port Glasgow 1863).

The *Tuskar* arrived at East Bute Docks Cardiff on 5 May 1889 (*South Wales Daily News*, 7 May 1889) and sailed for Liverpool on 7 May,

On 15 July he was discharged from the *Tuskar* at Liverpool. Described as Very good for both conduct and ability. Signed by John McPherson, Master. Witness was G Banister, 18 Postern St, Supt steward.

On 21 September 1889 he received a certificate from the Records of General Office of Shipping and Seamen, which listed some of his service up to then.

William Griffiths (1865-1959): Part 2: the 1890s

It seems that there may be a gap in the discharge papers available in Caernarfon Archives, as there is nearly a year between when he was discharged from the *Tuskar* on 15 July 1889, at Liverpool, and when he was engaged on the *Blencowie* on 14 June 1890 at Newcastle, as boatswain. *Blencowie*'s official number was 83,911, and was registered at Newcastle, 303 tons, 70 HP. The voyage was described as "Peruan", so it may be inferred that this was probably to the guano-producing areas such as the Chinchas Islands or Callao

On 12 July 1890 he was discharged from the *Blencowie*, at Cardiff. The Master was W Evans. He was described as very good for both ability and conduct. Yet bizarrely he was engaged as a boatswain on the same ship the very same day, on a voyage described as "foreign", and stayed on until he was discharged on 16 December.

On 13 February 1891 he was engaged on the *SS Runic* as an Able Seaman at Liverpool. The *SS Runic*'s official number was 93,837, built by Harland and Wolf of Belfast in 1889 of steel, and was registered at Liverpool, and 3,046 tons, 520 horsepower. The voyage was described as North Atlantic.

The *Runic* was a livestock carrier operated by the White Star Line, whose most famous ship is the ill-fated *Titanic*. The *SS Runic* was sold to the West India & Pacific SS Company in 1895 and renamed *Tampican*, and is not to be confused with the later White Star ship *Runic*, which was launched in 1900. He was discharged on 20 March at Liverpool, and described as very good for conduct and ability.

He appears on the 1891 census, on 1 April, at 82 Highfield Street, Liverpool, with his mother Jane and sister Catherine. Catherine is described as single, and her two daughters, Jane E, born 1879, and Annie, born 1881 appear on the census as daughters of Jane. This shows that Catherine, who was buried in 1908 at Edern, as Catherine Lancaster, had not yet married Mr Lancaster.

Jane had been widowed just over a year before, on 17 March 1890, and the £29 10/- left to her would not have left her comfortable by any means, but it seems that she was running a boarding house, since there were boarders who also had maritime connections. David Davies, Master Mariner, and his wife Ellen were born in Nefyn, so they almost certainly would not be strangers to the family. The other two boarders were Evan Morgan, aged 79, and Henry W Timothy, aged 19, both natives of Cardiganshire, another area with a strong maritime tradition.

On 17 July William engaged on the *Lake Ontario* at Liverpool, on a voyage to Montreal. SP *Lake Ontario*, official number 93,725 of Liverpool, had a registered tonnage of 2,922 tons, and engines of 400 horse power. He was discharged from the *Lake Ontario* on 14 August. The captain was H Campbell. William was described as very good for ability and conduct. On 21 August he was again engaged on the same ship as an Able Seaman, on another voyage to Montreal, and was discharged 18 September.

The *Lake Ontario* was 374.5ft long, had a beam width of 43.5ft, and clipper bow, two funnels and three masts, and was capable of 12 knots. It was clearly a passenger liner as it had accommodation for 200 first class passengers, 85 second and 1,000 third class. She had been built by J Lang of Sunderland and was launched on 10 March 1887, for the Beaver Line.

The Beaver Line, formed in 1867 as the Canada SS Company, sailed from Liverpool to Quebec and Montreal, and also owned the *Lake Erie*, *Lake Michigan* and *Lake Huron*. The company, named for the Beaver on its flag, also inaugurated a service to New York in 1881, but was liquidated in 1894. William was again engaged on the *Lake Ontario* on 25 September on a voyage to Montreal, and was discharged 24 October at Liverpool.

On 1 January 1892 he was engaged on the *Blencowie* as a boatswain, in the coasting trade, and on 9 April was discharged at Penarth, near Cardiff. Master was W Evans. Witness Owen Roberts, Chief Mate of *Blencowie*.

On 11 June he was engaged on the *Lake Ontario* at Liverpool, as an Able Seaman, on a voyage to Montreal. On his discharge paper on 8 July he is named as William Lloyd.

On 16 July he was again engaged at Liverpool on the *Lake Ontario* as an Able Seaman, on a voyage to Montreal, and was discharged on 13 August. It seems that the round trip from Liverpool to Montreal took just under a month, and that William would be on shore for a week between voyages. A ship with engines also had the advantage of not being dependent on favourable winds. The *Eleanor and Jane* in 1868 could take longer to do the relatively short journey from Dublin to Bristol, leaving Dublin on 29 December 1867, and arriving at Bristol on 29 January 1868, probably due to adverse winds.

After 13 August 1892 William entered the *Princess Maud*, as an Able Seaman. The *SS Princess Maud*, 90,023 of Glasgow, had a registered tonnage of 298. This voyage was in the Home Trade, and William was discharged from her on 3 November. The master was Archibald Kerr. The witness was Donald McNicol, chief officer of the *Princess Maud*.

On 11 January 1893 he entered the *Swan* as a seaman. The *Swan*, a steam ship built in Newcastle in 1867, had the official number 56,061 of Liverpool, and a registered tonnage of 427. William had no fund ticket. He was discharged on 13 December at Liverpool. The certificate was dated December 20. The Master was John Edwards.

He was obviously ashore on 24 March 1893, because on that date he married Ellen Thomas at Victoria Chapel, Great Crosshall Street, by licence, by the rites and ceremonies of the Welsh Calvinistic Methodists. Ellen was the daughter of Richard and Emma Thomas of Pentre Garreg Bach, Benllech, Anglesey. William gives his address as 82 Highfield Street.

Ellen gives her address as Llanfairmathafarneithaf, Anglesey, but it could be that she was then in Liverpool acting as housekeeper for her brothers: William, Owen and Richard who were builders in Liverpool, and are mentioned in *The Welsh Builder on Merseyside*. After a time in South Africa, the brothers returned to Liverpool where Richard died, and was buried at Longmoor Lane on 11 January 1907, but William and Owen emigrated to Canada.

On 3 January 1894 he was engaged on the *Swan* as an Able Seaman in the Home Trade, and on 8 March he was discharged at Liverpool. The certificate was dated March 9. The captain was E Short, and the witness was S Williams, mate of *SS Swan*. William gives his place of birth as St Dogmael's, whereas in all his other papers, Nevin or Caernarfonshire are consistently put down. There is no known connection with the Cardigan area to explain this aberration.

On 11 April he entered the *Martin* as an Able Seaman. The *Martin* of London, official number 73,554 (registered in 1875), 469 tons, was engaged in the home trade. On 7 May he was discharged from the *Martin* at Manchester. The Master was C Meoles. Witness was J Bollen, on board, mariner.

On 26 May he was engaged on the *Lake Ontario* at Liverpool as an Able Seaman, on a voyage to Quebec and Montreal and was discharged 23 June. The Master was H Campbell. William's conduct and ability were described as very good.

The pattern of a round trip of just under a month, with a week ashore between voyages is confirmed by the next two voyages on the *Lake Ontario*, with William being engaged as an Able Seaman again on 30 June, being discharged on 28 July, and engaged again on 4 August, and being discharged 21 August, again both voyages being to Quebec and Montreal, and the captain again being H Campbell.

On the 28 August he was engaged on a much smaller steam ship, the *SS Warrenpoint*, of Newry, of a mere 71 tons, which was involved in the coasting trade.

He was discharged from her on 8 September 1894. The Master was Allin Swift, and the witness was Robert McPhee of 107 Chapple Street, Newry.

There is a gap in the discharge papers available after 1894 until 1905. In 1900 William and Ellen lived at 29 Beech Grove, Elm Road, Seaforth, just north of Bootle, and two of their daughters were buried at Toxteth Park cemetery on 19 April 1900, namely Ellen Prydderch Griffiths, aged 21 months, and Annie Mary Griffiths aged 5 months, Buried in section E156, by the Rev Thomas Evans.

..

William Griffiths (1865-1959): 20th Century

William Griffiths was living in Seaforth in 1900, and had been living in the Liverpool area for years before, since so many of his voyages since at least 1891 start at Liverpool. As well as the two infant daughters buried at Toxteth Park cemetery, he also had Gwilym, Emma, Owen, Jenny and John Richard Griffiths, who was born at Seaforth on 16 July 1901.

The 1901 census for Seaforth shows a William Griffiths, aged 35 born in Nevin, who was a "builders timekeeper", and married to Ellen, aged 31, born in Anglesey. This is quite an unexpected departure from his work as a mariner. The fact his brothers-in-law were builders might explain this. It seems that a builder's timekeeper's role was to ensure that the workers turned up on time, and to keep a tally of the hours they actually worked. Perhaps this temporary change of occupation is the explanation for the gap in the discharge certificates between 1894 and 1905.

By 1904 the family had moved to Tyddyn Fadog, a farm in Benllech, which was the home of relatives of Ellen. Being near to Bangor rather than Liverpool would seem to be the reason for William's long connection with the Port Penrhyn slate ships, and on 10 October 1905 he was engaged on the *SS Harrier* at Portdinorwic. The *SS Harrier* was registered at Beaumaris, official number 102,768. She was built in Bowling, near Dumbarton, Scotland in 1893, and was registered at Beaumaris in 1894, and belonged to Lord Penrhyn. Its length was 120ft, breadth 20ft, depth of hull 9ft4, net tonnage 69, and gross tonnage 207. The horsepower of her engine was 50. The *Harrier,* and her sister ship the *Bangor*, which William served on, belonged to the Anglesey Shipping Company, which was originally owned by a group of English businessmen, with a Welsh manager, O T Jones of Erw Fair, Bangor. The Anglesey Shipping Company was later taken over by the Penrhyn slate quarries, and O T Jones remained as the manager.

The only crew lists available at Llangefni archives for the *Harrier* during William's time of service are those for 1906 and 1913, but it can be taken that those two years are a reasonable sample of the *Harrier*'s voyages. Certainly the list of ports visited and the nature of the voyages are remarkably similar.

In both years the managing owner was O T Jones of Erw Fair, Bangor, and the Master was Hugh Jones of 5 William Street, Bangor. The crew lists on the ship in both years (seven years apart) are almost identical, with Hugh Jones, William Pritchard (Mate), David Hughes (AB), William Griffith (AB) Owen Parry (Engineer) all appear in both years. William Nicholson (Second Engineer) and Thomas Griffiths (Fireman) appear in 1906, but in 1913 they have been replaced by Evan Williams (Second Engineer), and William Williams (Fireman), and on March 15 1913 Evan Williams and David Hughes left, and were replaced by Thomas Lewis, but by July 1913 David Hughes was back on the *Harrier*. This would suggest a remarkable stability in the crew, with little desire to jump ship.

It would be tedious and repetitive to list the voyages, but it seems that the general pattern was to transport slates from Bangor to ports in Ireland (including Belfast, Dublin, Dingle, Londonderry, Dundalk), Scotland (including Bowling, Inverness and Irvine), South Wales, the Isle of Man, western England (including Silloth, Liverpool, Preston, Gloucester), and return to Bangor, probably with coal if the port of call was in South Wales, but a lot of the return voyages from Dublin, Larne, Coleraine, Irvine, Belfast, Bowling, Gloucester and Preston are described as "light", meaning there was no suitable cargo for the return journey. This also happened occasionally, but less frequently with Cardiff and Liverpool, where cargoes of coal could be expected. Frustratingly the cargoes actually carried are never described.

Voyages from Bangor were not described as "light" except for one exception. On 16 January 1913 the *Harrier* sailed light from Bangor to Portdinorwic, which is another slate port, but this would seem bizarre when Bangor itself was an important slate port. One clue is that the *Harrier* was apparently there for a long time as she then sailed light from Portdinorwic to Bangor on 9 February. The log does not actually shed any light on the reason for this seemingly pointless voyage, but it may be that the

Harrier was being repaired.

There is another lengthy time at port, in Liverpool, in November 1913. The *Harrier* had left Bangor on 13 November and arrived at Liverpool on 14 November, but did not leave Liverpool until 29 November, and that was light. This raises the question of whether this may also be a repair.

Safety seems to have been an important issue on the *Harrier* in 1913, as the log makes fairly frequent mentions of a "brat drill", and of the life-saving appliances being examined.

One advantage with a ship which made short, relatively local voyages, rather than the longer ocean-going ones, is that it was possible to spend Christmas at home, and this does seem to be the case with the *Harrier*. In 1906 the Harrier arrived from Belfast on 25 December, and departed for Belfast on 27 December, and likewise in 1913, arrived from Belfast on 24 December, and departed 27 December for Cardiff.

He served on the *Harrier* until 15 January 1916, when he was discharged at Bangor. The master was Hugh Jones; the witness was William Hughes, mariner, of Port Penrhyn.

He received a glowing reference dated 28 January 1916:

Telegrams Jones, Erwfair, Bangor. Tel no 142. After 5pm no 44. Port Penrhyn, Bangor, North Wales. This is to certify that Mr William Griffith, Tyddyn Tirion, Tynygongl, Anglesey, has served as able seaman in the *SS Harrier* for the past 10 years and 3 months, during the whole of which time it is reported to me that he has given every satisfaction as regards ability and conduct. He is a total abstainer and can be recommended to anyone requiring his services. He left the vessel of his own accord.

He seems to have had a brief spell of serving again on Liverpool ships, as on 6 July 1916 he was engaged on the *Pride of Weaver* at Liverpool. The *Pride of Weaver,* official number 110,530 of Liverpool, 77 tons, was engaged in the home trade. William had no RNR commission or certificate.

On 6 August William was discharged from the *Pride of Weaver* at Liverpool. Witness WJ Brown, Engineer of 48 Warrington Road, Widnes.

On 8 May 1917 he was engaged on the *Jennie* at Garston. The *SS Jennie*, official number 118,004 of Liverpool, 87 tons, 33 horsepower, was engaged in the coasting trade. On 18 June 1917 he was discharged from the *Jennie* at Holyhead. The Master was John Hughes. Witness was William Hughes, Mate of 12 Llaneilian Road, Amlwch.

On 12 July 1917 he was engaged on the *SS Clwyd* at Mostyn as an Able Seaman.

The *SS Clwyd*, official number 127,956 of Liverpool, 124 tons, 45 horsepower, was also involved in the coasting trade.

On 21 December 1917 he was discharged from the Clwyd at Douglas. The Master was John Jones, and the witness was Llewelyn Griffiths, Mate of 11 Garth Road, Bangor. The newspaper reports soon after show that this was not just a calm discharge at the end of a voyage, but rather as a result of their ship being sunk in a collision off the Skerries, and being on a small boat for 40 hours, in the kind of harsh weather that can be expected in the Irish Sea in December. If we consider that this was during the First World War, then the experience would have been even more frightening due to the risk of U-boats patrolling the Irish Sea, though the newspaper reports quoted don't refer to this further danger.

Y Dinesydd Cymreig of 26 December 1917 refers to a report from Lloyd's of the *Clwyd*, a 289 ton steamer from Chester having been sunk in a collision with an unknown steamer on December 19, and the crew, consisting of six men, plus the dead chief engineer, being landed in port after having been rescued by a trawler.

The *South Wales Weekly Post* gives a bit more information, but describes the *Clwyd* as a Swansea trading steamer:

CHIEF ENGINEER DIES IN BOAT. Plight of Swansea Trader's Crew. Six members of the crew of the Swansea trading steamer *Clwyd* have been landed after being in a small boat for forty hours. The steamer sank off Skerries, Anglesey, after a collision with an unknown vessel. The crew of seven pulled for Preston, but were driven to sea by the wind and tide, and an attempt to reach Barrow was also unsuccessful. The chief engineer died in the boat. The men were without food, and had to drink rain water caught in a piece of canvas. They were eventually picked up, completely exhausted, off the Isle of Man.

The *North Wales Chronicle*, quite naturally gives the local angle of the lost ship being a North Wales coasting steamer:

LOSS OF A NORTH WALES COASTING STEAMER. CREW 36 HOURS IN OPEN BOAT. A sad tale of the sea was disclosed at an inquest at Douglas, on Saturday, concerning the death of William Owen Jones (47), chief engineer of the steamer *Clwyd*, which was on a voyage from Dublin to Point of Air. The *Clwyd* when off the Skerries, near Holyhead, on Wednesday week, was struck on the starboard side by an unknown steamer. It was very dark at the time, and a heavy sea was running. The vessel was so badly holed that the crew of seven took to the boats. The other steamer was not seen by them after the impact, and there was no response to their distress signals, which were kept going for half an hour. There was neither food nor water in the small boat, and many of the men were only partly clad. They drifted, about for 36 hours, suffering terribly, before they were picked up by the trawler *Fly*, of Fleetwood, and taken to Douglas. Jones died from exposure eight hours before reaching port. The Captain of the *Fly* described the condition of the men as simply shocking. When his vessel sighted the small boat a most pitiable sight met their gaze. He said "It was with difficulty that we got the six men from the boat; they were so numbed with the cold that they could not help themselves. They were quite stiff."

After such a traumatic experience, it would be natural to expect him to have a fairly long rest to recover, so that might be the explanation why there is rather a long gap before the next extant record of a voyage, when he was engaged on the *SS Bangor* in 1922.

We know from the electoral register that in 1919 William lived at Tyddyn Tirion, Benllech.

On 10 January 1922 he was engaged on the *SS Bangor* at Bangor as an Able Seaman. The *SS Bangor*, 101,752, of Beaumaris, 340 tons, 72 horsepower, was involved in the coasting trade. She was a sister ship of the *Harrier*, and he remained on her until 27 September 1929 when he was discharged from her at Bangor. The master was William Williams. The witness to his discharge paper was W Pritchard, Mate, of 17 Mount Street, Menai Bridge.

When the *Harrier* was sold to South Africa, William was offered the opportunity, which he turned down, of being on the crew taking her there. The *Harrier* was registered at Cape Town, South Africa in 1928. The Harrier's account book for 1927, available at Caernarfon Archives shows that her typical cargoes included coal to Garston and Barrow, slates to Belfast, Waterford, Liverpool and Newcastle, and writing slates to Belfast and Dublin. The *Bangor*'s cargoes and ports of call would almost certainly have been the same.

William Griffiths later moved to Bryn Llan, Benllech, and died in 1959, and was buried at Llaneugrad cemetery. The *Holyhead Chronicle* 1 May 1959 gives the obituary for William Griffiths.

"On Wednesday week at Llaneugrad the funeral took place of Mr William Griffiths, Bryn Llan, who was 94. He was a native of Morfa Nefyn and spent his earlier years at sea, and lived at Tyddyn Tirion previous to moving to Bryn Llan.

Chief mourners were Mrs E Clarke (daughter), Mr and Mrs JR Griffiths, councillor and Mrs OJ Griffiths (sons and daughters in law), Mr Gwilym Griffiths (son)."

Useful Websites

Crew List Index Project (CLIP): http://www.crewlist.org.uk. (This has lots of information on the sources of information on mariners and ships, and useful links to online indexes such as Reg Davies's Welsh Mariners, and Lloyd's Captains List, and can therefore be regarded as a portal to more information)

Welsh Newspapers Online: http://newspapers.library.wales (This fully searchable website allows access to Welsh newspapers from 1804 to 1919, and thus the Shipping Intelligence columns, which were a great feature of 19th century newspapers, and also of reports of more dramatic events such as shipwrecks)

Rhiw.com: http://www.rhiw.com (Despite the name, this website covers the whole of Llŷn, not just Rhiw, and has a good section on the seafaring tradition of the area).

Llŷn Maritime Museum: http://www.llyn-maritime-museum.co.uk/ (This museum, housed in a former church, tells the rich maritime story of Nefyn and the surrounding district).

Background Reading

Maritime Wales: Caernarfon,Gwynedd Archives and Museum Services. Annual since 1976, has scholarly articles on aspects of Welsh maritme history.

Eames, Aled: Ventures in Sail, Caernarfon, Gwynedd Archives and Museum Services, 1987. Gives an account of various aspects of maritime trade in Gwynedd, and the links to Liverpool.

Thomas, David, (edited by Evans, Robin), Hen Longau Sir Gaernarfon, Llanrwst, Gwasg Carreg Gwalch, 2007. This is a revised version of an old Welsh-language classic on the old ships of Caernarfonshire.

Printed in Great Britain
by Amazon